# How to Write a Book That Doesn't Suck (and Will Actually Sell)

## The Ultimate, No B.S. Guide to Writing a Non-Fiction Book

by Michael Rogan
Editor, Indie Pub Nation

Published in USA by: Indie Pub Nation

Michael Rogan

© Copyright 2019

ISBN-13: 978-1-970119-37-4
ISBN-10: 1-970119-37-3

# Table of Contents

# Also By Michael Rogan

Kindle Publishing Made (Stupidly) Easy

How to Make a Damn Good Living When Self-Publishing a Book

Screw You, Writer's Block

Lazy Writer's Guide to Twitter

Lazy Writer's Guide to Pinterest

# About the Author

Michael Rogan is a former Hollywood screenplay reader, traditional publishing editor and founder of Indie Pub Nation - an inbox periodical devoted to helping authors spread their message (and get paid while doing it.)

His mission in life to rid the world of books about whiny teenage vampires who play baseball.

# A Special FREE Gift for You!

If you'd like FREE instant access to my seminar "5 Secrets to Making a Damn Good Living (As a Writer)" then head over to **IndiePubNation.com/5secrets**. (What else you gonna do? Read another "Twilight" book?!)

4

# Prologue: Why It's the Best Time Ever to Write That Damn Book of Yours

*"Yes, it's hard to write. But it's harder not to."*
*-Carl Doren*

Ten years ago you and I wouldn't be having this conversation.

I'd STILL be spending my days writing horrible, SEO-optimized 500-word articles about hair loss remedies and lower-back Celtic tattoos and the fascinating world of discount prom dresses.

I'd STILL be sending out pallets of query letters to New York publishing houses hoping a bright, ambitious junior literary agent would read my written pleas and bestow me a three-book contract, right away.

And I'd STILL be spending my weekends slouched over a laptop, wondering if I would EVER do what I've wanted to do since I was that awkward, shy kid on the school bus who was scared to talk to girls and kept his nose in buried in the Dune Chronicles…

Have people read the words I wrote. (And pay me for them.)

But then something amazing happened.

A little start-up based out of Seattle, that started out by selling CDs from obscure, niche bands that nobody had ever heard of, somehow transformed itself into not just a global e-commerce giant…

…but into an earth-shaking MEDIA company who changed the way all of us read. (And write.)

I won't try to convince you the Kindle is our generation's Gutenberg Bible. (Though I think it is.)

But I will say Amazon and its HUGE inventory, streamlined infrastructure, and wealth of customer reviews — it's most valuable asset — has not just legitimized self-publishing…

**It's also legitimized YOU.**

Legitimized your right to call yourself a writer, expert, thought leader, teacher, philosopher, thinker, blogger, consultant, coach, raving political fanatic, paranoid conspiracy theorist or whatever else you are in this new twenty-first-century economy.

If you get nothing else from this book, realize, for the first time since the 18th century, the ONLY thing standing between you and the income, prestige and status that comes from being a full-time, professional writer…

Are the words you write. (Not the agency that represents you or the New York publishing house that distributes your work.)

And unless you're a Wiley or a Simon & Schuster, that makes these exciting days.

# Why the Hell Should You Listen Anyway?

Because I've made every mistake a self-published non-fiction author can make.

I've written dozens of books that had no marketplace viability. (Who doesn't want a three-volume set about how to collect "Magic: The Gathering" cards?)

I've started many projects only to find out halfway-through that the material and the intended readership bored the crap out of me...

And I've agonized over countless outlines, index cards and treatments trying to find that magic formula that would unlock the secret to a killer book.

And through much trial — and a crap load of error — and having self-published over twenty-five non-fiction books on good, old Amazon, I have learned one important thing.

Writing a non-fiction book is EASY. Writing a non-fiction book people will buy is a BIT tougher.

But neither are impossible, nor difficult.

The key is to have a system. A structure.

An organized approach that lets you do LESS thinking about what you will write, and more actual get-down-to-it WRITING.

And that's why I wrote this book.

I WANT to show you the exact system I used to organize, research and write every single one of my published non-fiction books. (Most of them completed in less than two weeks.)

I'll point out many of the obstacles and self-sabotage traps to avoid along the way. These are the traps that can derail your creative journey to published manuscript.

I will give you my insider strategies for making the HUGE trans-formative leap from hobbyist-wannabe to professional working writer.

Because that's what I want. To help you (finally) become a professional writer.

So YOU can spend your days coming up with new, interesting ways to share your knowledge, insight, perspective and personality with the world. (And not stuck in some crappy, dead-end job where your only respite is ten days of paid vacation… if you're lucky.)

The best thing about this system is, you don't have to be:

- An amazing writer
- A college graduate
- An avid reader
- A person with tons of free time
- An expert in your field

All you have to have is SOMETHING to say. It'll be my job to show you HOW to say it.

Shall we begin your quest to non-fiction book world domination?

# Chapter 1:

# Super-Ninja Secrets to Making a Living From Your Books

*"You must not suppose, because I am a man of letters, that I never tried to make an honest living."*
*-George Bernard Shaw*

There is a metric crap load of self-published books on Amazon. (Nearly 400,000 published each year.)

But before you freak out and think "Oh My God, I'll never be able to write a non-fiction book that stands out in a crowded marketplace like that."

"I might as well give up on my dream, move

back in with my parents, and get that teaching credential everyone says I should."

Breathe. Relax. And realize: most self-published books suck.

I don't mean kinda bad. Or sorta awful.

I don't mean they're filled with crappy formatting (which most of them are) or an awkward, overwrought prose style (which is the norm) or the shittiest book cover you will ever see.

No, most of the books self-published on Amazon suffer from one fatal flaw: the author doesn't GIVE a shit about the topic.

The secret to making a REAL LIVING as a professional writer can be boiled down to THREE steps:

- Write a book about something you care about
- Write more than one book
- Publish it in eBook form

# The Myth of the Expert

Notice I said nothing about being an expert, or about having a Ph.D., or having read EVERY single book written on a subject.

Those things are liabilities. One of the biggest strengths I have as a non-fiction writer, besides my dashing good looks and dreamy eyes, is my ability to explain (somewhat) difficult concepts and ideas like somebody who is NOT an expert.

Because, in every book I've written I'm not an expert. (I'm simply a guy researching and writing on a topic that captures him while doing best to cut out all the boring technical crap.)

Weird thing is: by writing a book as a non-expert you become an expert. (Which can be a HUGE career changer. But more on that later.)

# The Myth of the Overnight Bestseller

Unfortunately realizing your dream of being a

professional writer isn't accomplished by writing ONE book and waiting for the world to gush over your talents.

The truth is: you will NEVER, EVER make a living with a single book.

Sorry, Salinger. It's too damn hard to promote a single book. (Or get a big enough readership by peddling one piece of content written by an unknown author.)

I know. Because I've tried.

I tried the whole "writing a HUGE epic that covers every single aspect of a specific topic" to make me the go-to resource in my unstoppable climb up the Amazon bestseller charts.

It doesn't work. That's because:

- **For non-fiction, people LIKE shorter books**. I shoot for a range of about 10,000-20,000 words per book.
- **People want focused, narrow books on a single topic**. Not huge

compendiums that cover every problem. That's for the huge hardcover reference guide or "Dummies" book; not something for the newbie self-publisher.

- **It's easier to promote three to five small books, than one HUGE tome**.
- **Having three to five books, in a single category, as opposed to one HUGE book, helps you dominate** your Kindle category. (Especially in the Amazon "Customers Also Bought" section.)

## The Myth of the Printed Book

This is the part where you point out I'm a total idiot, and that a non-fiction volume that's 10,000 words long is FAR too short for a "real" book. Especially one that'll make it to print.

And you're right, if this was 1997.

But having brought more than 35 books to print, I can tell you that:

- People like shorter, smaller non-fiction books

- People tend to buy BOTH the print **and eBook copies of** books they lik**e**

- **People t**end to FINISH shor**ter, smaller** non-fiction books (Meaning they're more likely to get to that call-to-action stuff in the back of your book.)

So, before you have a nervous breakdown over the prospect of writing THREE books, let alone a single book, remember: you're not penning *Anna Karenina.*

These are short "books" of 75-100 pages — double spaced — that cover a specific topic. (Examples include - *Facebook advertising, kitchen cabinet refinishing, Betta fish breeding;* these do NOT include broad topics such as s*ocial media, cabinetry, fish care.*)

When competitively priced — I recommend a starting sale price of $.99 and then working your way up to $2.99 when you've got five or more reviews — and combined with other books in a series, it's possible to dominate your non-fiction market in two months.

As long as you find a subject you care about. And that's what the next chapter is all about.

# Chapter 1 Key Takeaways:

- **Most self-published books suck.** Don't freak out over the competition. There ain't that much.

- **The key to success is to write more than one book about a subject you have an interest in.** Don't write for profits, write for passion.

- **You don't have to be an expert to write a book about something.** In fact, being an expert can be to your detriment.

- **Skip the printed book market, at least until you're an established author.** Preparing your book for print publication takes far too much time, energy and money to worry about.

# Chapter 2:

# Yeah, But What the Hell Am I Going to Write About?

*"The greatest thing in this world is not where we are, but in what direction we are going."*
—*Oliver Wendell Holmes*

Think you'll NEVER come up with an interesting book topic?

Want to write a book but don't know what the hell to write about? (Or what a book idea looks like?)

Fear not, intrepid non-fiction writer, the topic for your next fabulous book project is just minutes away! (Maybe seconds, depending on your caffeine level.)

So, here are my Top 7 Strategies for Finding a Killer Book Topic that's interesting, personal — doesn't require a ton of research — and may pet you up for a dazzling full-time career as a working writer:

## Strategy No.1: Crap You Know Other People Don't

Everybody knows something.

Everybody.

Even my cousin, who's forty-three years old and has never had a job, never filed a tax return, and has never lived five miles outside of his hometown, knows SOMETHING. (In his case, that hi acquiring vintage 70s toy collectibles. If ya got an original Planet of the Apes action figure, I'll give you his number.)

And if he can write a book about that, which he has, then I'm damn sure there's something you KNOW somebody would like to know.

Can be almost anything: how to set up a blog, how to build a chicken coop, how to run a 5k, how to create an herb garden, how to NOT kill those annoying drivers in the lane next to you when they piss you off.

It doesn't matter if it seems simple, or that people could find the information somewhere else. You're saving them time by organizing the knowledge into and digestible form. (And for that, people will pay you money.)

**Action Step:** *Make a list of ten to fifteen things you know how to do, that somebody else might have difficulty understanding. (Dig deep; go beyond the usual stuff.)*

## Strategy No.2: Your Biggest Obstacles/Challenges

Nothing sells a non-fiction book like experience. There's something about the whole "I've been to hell and back again" school of writing that lends serious credibility and authority to your books. (And can transform your how-to volume from a modest-selling tome to an industry standard.)

I talk to newbie non-fiction writers all the time SITTING on goldmines of valuable life experience. (And don't even know it.)

So ask yourself: what kick-ass and huge obstacles have I gone through in my life?

- An alcoholic father?
- Bankruptcy?
- Divorce?
- Chronic pain?
- An addiction to smartphone games involving fruit?

That you're reading these words means you've survived some serious crap-ola. And it doesn't have to be as dramatic as the list above.

I have a friend who went through the stressful, agonizing process of getting a home loan modification from Wells Fargo Bank. (An effort worthy of a Greek epic poem.) His one book on that topic brings him an easy $1,000 a month, doing zero promotion for it.

*Action Step: Make a list of the top 5 biggie life obstacles you've overcome. (And don't forget: surviving IS overcoming.)*

# Strategy No.3: What You're Already Into

Want to know the easiest way to find a topic for your non-fiction book?

Look at:

- Books on your bookshelf
- Magazines you read
- Websites you visit
- TV shows you watch
- Message boards you visit

Chances are, you already spend a good deal of time reading, watching, and consuming material related to a subject that'd make for a fabulous book topic. (This is my number one, go-to way for coming up with book topics.)

*Do you like to read model train magazines?* Well maybe you could write a set of books on how to find, restore and build model trains.

*Do you like to refinish second-hand furniture?* Well, then you could do a series of guides on buying and restoring furniture on the weekends.

*Are you into triathlons?* (If you are, you could do a series of books on training, running and recovering from triathlon events.)

The best part about this strategy is you don't have to be an expert. You just have to be interested.

And by doing research for the books you'll be learning more about something you already care about. Win-win!

*Action Step: Look at all the books, magazines, TV shows, and websites you check out often. Make a list of ten topics that interest you and could make for interesting book subjects.*

## Strategy No.4: What People are Writing Crappy Articles About

Think the self-published fare on Amazon is total crap? It's Nobel Prize-winning level when compared to the sludge on that content farm known as <u>Ezine Articles</u>.

For those not acquainted with the low-grade web content mill that is Ezine Articles, it's an article directory where people "write" 400-word articles about a HUGE variety of topics.

And most of them are awful.

They are usually designed to sell crappy Internet Marketing products or build backlinks to somebody's horrible blog. (I should know because, in my old job, I'd write them to promote crappy Internet Marketing products and build backlinks.)

Many how-to self-publishing guides recommend you use Ezine Articles for book research. This is like using Facebook comments as a basis for your Ph.D. thesis. Not a good idea.

But Ezine Articles ARE fantastic for finding broad and specific categories you could write a book on. All you do is hover over the article categories, then go a-hunting for topics.

In the Health & Fitness category alone there are interesting sub-topics such as anxiety, back pain, detoxification, meditation, and phobias.

The possibilities are endless. Make sure you stick to the headlines as inspiration; we wouldn't want any of that awful writing to rub off on you.

*Action Step: Scan Ezine Articles for topics. Come up with at least ten topics you have SOME background or interest in.*

# Strategy No. 5: What People are Publishing on Amazon

A lot of how-to writing guides recommend you do a majority of your topic research in the Amazon book categories.

I'm lukewarm about this strategy; I tend to be one of those writers who gets overwhelmed and intimidated by seeing a crowded book category.

That said: if there's more than a handful of books about a specific topic in the Amazon inventory that means there IS an audience for it.

The most important tool is the left-hand navigation, where the Kindle Bookstore organizes its vast book catalog. By simply following the Kindle rabbit hole you'll get a sense of where the readers are. (And aren't.)

For example: under the large category "Parenting & Relationships" I see that the sub-category "Family Health" has 32 titles. The "Special Needs" sub-category has 2,100 titles.

And if you keep digging, you'll see that in the "Disabilities" sub-category, "Autism" and "ADD" are well represented. (But "Bi-polar," "Depression" and "Dyslexia"…not so much.)

Not that you couldn't write a book about childhood bi-polar or dyslexia, just that you may encounter an uphill battle finding an audience. (Better to be a small fish in a big pond, than be a big fish in a pond with no water, or buyers.)

*Action Step: Peruse the Amazon Kindle book categories and find five topics, that already have books representing them, that you could see yourself writing a book about.*

## Strategy No.6: Magazines Already Being Published

Lots of would-be non-fiction writers spend hours combing through the Kindle bookstore category listings, looking for that latest, trendy book topic to help them conquer the world. But they often skip over one of the best book idea resources

Amazon offers: the <u>Magazine Subscriptions</u> page.

This comprehensive list of periodicals — 8,100 in "Professional and Trade" alone! — can give you some real out-of-the box ideas you might never have thought of.

Did you know there are magazines devoted to subjects such as?

- Arabian horses
- Spinning yarn
- The pest control industry
- Pontoons & Deck boats
- Rubber stamping
- Figure skating
- 4WD Toyota Trucks

I don't know if you've ever worked in the magazine biz — I had a brief stint which went about as well as my triathlon career — but it is difficult, expensive and rewarding work. (Which most publishers would not attempt if they weren't DAMN sure there was some kind of audience for the magazine.)

*Action Step: Browse through the comprehensive Amazon magazine subscription results. Find five topics you find interesting and would like to learn more about.*

# Strategy No.7: Your Favorite Section of the Bookstore

Sometimes the simplest strategy is the best.

For a brief time, after I was "invited" by my previous employer to "explore" other employment options, I tried my hand at writing mini-guides to such exciting topics as: How to Run a 5K, Triathlon Recovery Tips, and Century-Ride Strategies. (Yeah, it's about as fun as it sounds.)

Thing was: when I entered a bookstore, the endurance sports section was the LAST section I would be caught dead in.

Instead I headed straight for:

- Reference (Where all the writing books were)
- Film (Where all the screenwriting books were)
- Business/Social Media (Because I like money)
- Sci-Fi/Fantasy (Because I have the emotional maturity of a twelve-year-old)

And the moment I followed my OWN interests, instead of writing about what I THOUGHT I should write about, was when I started to make money at this whole writing thing.

*Action Step: Head to the bookstore and tote the four or five sections that interest you the most. Browse the books on the shelf and come up with two or three topics per section you could add to your book idea list.*

# Chapter 2 Key Takeaways:

- **Start with making a list of the skills and knowledge you already have.** Pay particular attention to any previous training or past job experience you could spin into a book or two.

- **Make a list of the biggest obstacles you've faced in your life.** Did you learn something from them you could organize in book form?

- **Look at the stuff you already read, watch and listen to for ready-made book ideas.** Don't worry if you're not an expert, you just have to be interested.

- **Browse the categories in the article directory, Ezine Articles, for topics.** Don't read the articles…they are horrible.

- **Check out the various book categories in the Kindle Bookstore.**

Don't get scared off by too much competition but proceed with caution over ideas in which there are few books at all.

- **Scan the magazine subscriptions page on Amazon**. If somebody publishes a magazine about it, that means it's a worthy book topic.

- **Head to your favorite sections at your local bookstore**. Look through the stacks to see if it sparks any ideas for book topics you could tackle.

# Chapter 3:

# The 3 Pillars to Finding a Kick-Ass Non-Fiction Book Idea

*"You don't need to be the best at what you do, you just need to be the only one."*

*-Jerry Garcia*

Writing a book is nice.

Writing a book that total strangers will buy separates wannabe scribblers from professional writers.

You'll want to skip this chapter. You'll figure:

"I've got my killer book topic… I'm ready to go!"

Please, oh please, don't do this.

Trust me: if I could jump in my Amazon Kindle time machine and head back to the time before I spent weeks and months researching, planning and writing books that nobody wanted to read AND contributed nothing to anyone's life…

I would do it in a heartbeat.

Because this chapter is all about saving you TIME. I'm confident following the strategies in this book will help you write a kick-ass book. (We just want to make sure there's an actual audience for that kick-ass book when it's ready.)

So, grab your list of book topics, because you're about to put them through the THREE PILLARS of Kick-Ass Book Idea Awesomeness:

## Pillar No.1: Which Ideas Do I Need to Write About? (Now!)

This pillar isn't about which topics you know the

most about. Or which topics are related to your work history.

Or which idea you think will make you a million dollars. (*Spoiler alert*: The ideas you care the most about are the ones that make you the most money.)

Instead, look over your list and pick out five ideas you are MOST interested in writing NOW.

For years, I tried writing books I figured would be dead easy, from a research standpoint, to crank out. Turns out: nothing slows down the writing process like slugging through a topic that doesn't capture your imagination.

This doesn't mean you can't use your background or previous job for inspiration. People love to learn through stories, and your life experience is a great way to educate and point the way for your readers.

Don't marry a book topic if it's not something you REALLY are interested in writing at this moment.

*Action Step: Look over your master list of book topics.*

*Circle the top five ideas you're most enthusiastic about.*

# Pillar No.2: Which Ideas Have a Built-In Audience?

Though I hate the term "marketability" — sounds about as creative as an insurance seminar. It's good to know someone besides your Aunt Matilda will buy your book after you've published it.

And the easiest way to do that is to find out if there is a "market" for your book. Is there:

- A magazine devoted to your book topic?
- At least two to three books on Amazon related to your topic?
- A message board or website devoted to the topic?
- A Facebook page devoted to your topic? (There's a Facebook page devoted to everything)

- A clear demographic identifier for your ideal reader? (Women, realtors, martial artists, scrap bookers...female martial artist scrap bookers with a real estate license, etc.)

You want a reader to look at your book cover and say, "Hey, that's for me!"

And if you're not sure your book topic has a decent market to back it up, ask:

"Does this book topic help people save time, make money, feel better or do something cool or creative with their lives?"

If you can say YES, you're in good shape.

*Action Step: Look over your top five ideas and scratch any off the list that don't have a clear, identifiable audience. (Put an asterisk next to any book topic ideas that have a magazine or healthy number of books on Amazon.)*

# Pillar No. 3: Which Idea Will Change the World? (Somewhat)

Now, this pillar will sound new-agey, so bear with me. (Don't worry, I will not burn any incense.)

But I feel when somebody has a serious axe to grind or sees life from an alternative perspective CONTRARY to all the other bull crap that's out there...

...and then they write a book that takes on the establishment and gives voice to that maverick, hell-raising, rebellious part of themselves...

They find a readership, and a career, in NO time.

Couple years ago I wrote a series of books under the Punk Rock Marketing name that dealt with social media marketing.

Social media marketing? Yawn, right?

Except I wrote the books for people who HATE social media. (Like me.)

For people who think Twitter is a sign of the zombie apocalypse. (Like me.)

Who think social media is the modern version of your friends showing slides from their vacation to Disney World. (Just not as exciting!)

And while I did my research, and worked on my drafts, I had one dominant thought: most of what the social media gurus espouse is absolute horse shit.

Nobody cares about engagement or authenticity or "likes."

They care about making money and saving their businesses. And they want the LEAST they need to know to help them accomplish that.

Now, when I say "change" the world I don't mean you have to cure cancer or rid the world of Kardashian sister worship. (Though both would be nice.)

Instead, look at your topics and ask:

- "How can I bring something different to the table?"
- "What perspectives am I seeing (or not seeing) in the books and magazines

devoted to this topic?"

- "What needs saying, but isn't? And how can I be the one to say it?"

Approaching your book topic this way doesn't require advanced certification or years of experience in the field.

It requires passion and conviction. With those two in your pocket, you can write (and sell) a hell of a lot of books.

*Action Step: Browse through your list of top five book topics. Which topic would allow you to offer something unique and revolutionary to the table?*

**Disclaimer:** Before you write me an email saying "But, Michael, I have nothing new to say about my topic that can change the world," know WHAT you say may require some further research. (Which we'll cover in Chapter 4.) What's most important here is the NEED to say it. If ya got the need, then you'll find the kick-ass WHAT.

# Putting It All Together

So, how do you choose which idea to focus on? Well, here's something that might help: it doesn't matter.

Oh, sure, if you write a book about chicken coop maintenance and know nothing about chicken coops and care nothing about the subject…

Then, yeah, it MATTERS.

But in the big Kindle scheme of things, even if you spend a couple weeks researching and writing a book that does NOT become a New York Times bestseller, you'll still:

- Have a passive income asset that CAN bring in consistent revenue
- Learn a TON about the process of writing a non-fiction book
- Figure out if it's a topic you want to invest more time and energy into
- Get a bunch of confidence for your

next project (Because you've already
done it once)


So, pick the ONE topic that FEELS right. Now.
(And you can always tackle another topic at a later
date.)

# Chapter 3 Key Takeaways:

- **Look at your list of book topics and determine the top ones you are most interested in working on.** Enthusiasm and passion not only make the writing process more fun, but they make it a hell of a lot more marketable too.

- **Of your top book topics, see if there is a built-in audience in the form of a monthly magazine, many published books, or an identifiable demographic.** Most magazine publishers spend a ton of money on demographic research, so use it to your own advantage.

- **Choose the ONE book topic you feel will change the industry.** Ask how you can bring a perspective that's strong, passionate, opinionated and (somewhat) contrary to the majority.

# Chapter 4:

# Research Tips for People Who Hate Research

*"What we find changes who we become."*
*—Peter Morville*

Research for non-fiction writer newbies goes one of two ways:

**1) They LOVE research.** And spend months, if not years, devouring every single thing written about a subject. (And often end up NEVER getting around to finishing the book.)

**2) They SKIP research.** They find research boring and anti-creative and let their intuition take them all the way through.

Both approaches are dangerous. And both can derail your book project quicker than spilling a four-dollar latte on your laptop.

## Why Less is More

Months of in-depth research can be fun. And exhilarating. And make you feel like an honest-to-God writer, you know, without writing a single page.

But researching to this Puritan extent also violates a fundamental fact of the modern non-fiction reader: most people are lazy.

Oh sure, there are folks, like my uncle who likes to read one-thousand-page volumes about former presidents. (And pores over the footnotes like an accountant looking for refund opportunities.)

But, most people buying non-fiction books are asking themselves one simple question: "Which book will help me solve my problem — or educate me about this important topic — with the LEAST amount of effort from ME?"

They don't want every nuance, detail and theory about a topic. They need not have every assertion backed up with statistics and facts and census data.

They just want to KNOW what they NEED to know to get results. (And not much else.)

And your ability to explain the concepts and strategies in your book in a simple, conversational manner — without overwhelming the reader — is probably the number one factor in determining the success of your books.

## Why Research Kicks Serious Ass!

That being said, you still got to do your homework. Too often I'll read books from authors who've done little research beyond summarizing a few Ezine Articles — remember how dangerous those are — and copying a few blog posts they found on Technorati.

Following this path is a quick route to crappy

reviews and a high refund rate. Because readers may KNOW nothing about a specific book topic, but they'll damn well know if you're bluffing your way through with broad generalities and vague writing.

Because good research KILLS cliches!

We live in an age where everybody has plenty of crappy, unsolicited advice to offer. (Visit YouTube for the biggest crapfest factory of all time.)

Presenting correct and timely advice, in a manner that shows you know what the hell you're talking about, is a valuable asset that readers will connect to.

But it's hard to give correct and timely information to a reader, unless you're able to separate the compelling from the dated or obvious.

So, striking the perfect research balance is one of the first BIG challenges you'll face in your non-fiction book writing journey. I'm here to help with some tips to help you avoid the research blunders I've made.

So, here are my 6 Kick-Ass Research Sources to

help you become an "expert" in your field in less than a week:

## Kick-Ass Research Source No.1: The Kindle TOC Goldmine

This source is so easy it should be criminal. (And it might be.)

All you do is check out the top ten selling books in your given topic on Amazon and take a screenshot of their Table of Contents (TOC) page. (By clicking "See Inside" on the book listing page.)

Once you've got your screenshots gathered, write all the *Chapter Headings* and *Sub-Headings* in a word doc. By doing this you will discover:

- **How many chapters/sub-topics the authors feel they need to express their point**. This can range from six chapters to a monstrous thirty-two.

- **Which sub-topics the books include**. For instance: I did a book on job interviews, and it was damn clear from my research I'd have to include chapters on sample interview questions, phone interviews, and what to wear at the interview. (Even if I thought what you should wear was obvious.)

- **Which sub-topics are NOT in every book**. If you were writing a book on setting up living trusts, do you need to include a chapter on Wills? (Yeah, probably.) Paying off credit card debt after death? (Maybe not, according to the research.)

- **New ISSUES and problems you may not have thought of**. In my job interview book research, it surprised me to find video interviewing was a BIG topic that came up again and again. Good thing I did my research before writing, so

I didn't leave this crucial topic off the list.

- **How many pages are devoted to specific topics.** This isn't always scientific, but it'll give you a general sense of how much emphasis the authors are placing on certain chapter topics by looking at topic page counts.

The most comprehensive source for these Table of Contents info are the _For Dummies series_ and the _Idiot's Guide_ books. But be aware, you're using them for research.

Don't feel you have to include every topic these behemoths do. They are trying to be the ONE reference manual to rule them all. (A space you can't compete in.)

# Kick-Ass Research Source No.2: Top 2-3 Books in Your Topic

Oh, man... you mean, I'm going to ask you to read a frickin' book.

Not quite. This is where you get to master the art of scanning. (Most books are padded, making scanning an almost necessity.)

Here's what I do when canvassing books in my target field:

- **Grab two or three recent books on my subject**. I find them at the library or grab Kindle copies. (Because I'm cheap.)

- **Read the "Prologue" or "Introduction" and the first chapter**. This gives me a good sense of the author's tone, viewpoint, and big concerns. (As they see them.)

- **Write any Action Steps the authors advise**. Like the ones I have at the end of my chapters.

- **Go back and scan the book for any BIG points you might have missed**. These will be in the form of subheads or pull quotes.

- **Read the final chapter**. This (usually) provides the big takeaway the author hopes to impart to the reader.

Now, if you've got plenty of free time, and LOVE reading about your subject, then knock yourself out and read the whole books.

But don't spend too much time on this. You're looking for the MEAT. Because it's the meat people are paying you for. (And you'll discover how little meat most books have.)

# Kick-Ass Research Source No.3: Amazon Book Reviews

This might be my favorite method of research. Because NOBODY does it...and it's so DAMN helpful.

Now you aren't interested in the boring, generic "I loved this book! It was awesome," or the "I hate this book because it didn't get shipped on time."

You're looking for SPECIFIC points about the book:

- **What people thought was MISSING from the book**. This info alone is worth its weight in Amazon gold.

- **What people REALLY liked about the book**. Pay attention to adjectives readers use to describe the writing style and how information is presented. (People LOVE books that take them from confusion to clarity.)

- **What emotional hot-buttons the reviews bring up**. Readers will share personal stuff in these reviews. It's a good idea to think about how your information can help tie in to these powerful emotions. (Which is the REAL reason people buy stuff.)

- **Whether people felt misled or deceived by the title or cover**. This

happens more than you'd think.
Managing expectations is an important
part of writing your book.

- **Which topics were presented in an
overly simplistic or generic way.** This
is the most valuable part of reviews.
You'll figure out the "Yeah, no kidding"
topics you need to handle in a subtle, deft
way.

And, sometimes, you'll even get a full-on, head-
to-toe summary of a certain book. (Saves you the
trouble of having to read the damn thing.)

## Kick-Ass Research Source No.4:
## Google Alerts

I KNOW Google is taking over the world and
will implant a chip in our brains any day now…

But I LOVE all the FREE tools Google gives us
writers. I think my all-time favorite might be <u>Google</u>

<u>Alerts</u>.

In case you're not up on your Google World Domination Lingo, Google Alerts is a service which lets you create filters, or alerts that then email you web results for EVERYTHING published using certain parameters, such as keywords.

You can create alerts around things such as:

- **Content published using a specific phrase** - A "Facebook marketing" alert would give you everything using those two words

- **Content published from a specific source** - A "Olympics site: nytimes.com" alert would give you everything from the New York Times that includes the keyword "Olympics"

- **A single website and all its related websites** - "related: ChickenCoop.com" would give you all the similar web locations Google feels are in the same field as ChickenCoop.com

The possibilities are endless.

Now you'll want to be as specific as possible; setting up an alert around a single word, such as "Facebook," would send you every blog post, forum thread, and news article about Facebook. (Your inbox would get overrun.)

However, setting up these alerts, with precision, can be a great way to check in on the latest trends and happenings in your field. (Without having to read hundreds of blogs and Facebook pages a day.)

# Kick-Ass Research Source No.5: Message Boards

I know what you're thinking… message boards? You mean those places where unstable people abuse each other over which DSLR camera is the best? (Canon is the best DSLR, hands down.)

Yeah, that's true. Forums and message boards

can be fantastic little petri dishes of dysfunction and the ills of having too much free time…

But they can also be FANTASTIC sources of research. Because it's in forums where people ask questions. ("How do I fill in my backyard pool?" "How do I become a plus size model?" "What's the best way to stop the Kardashian sisters from taking over the world?")

Here's how I recommend you approach your message board research:

- **Find two or three boards related to your topic**. If you don't know of any, enter "[your topic] AND forum" enter your Google search box.

- **Look through each board and find the most popular posts.** These will be made "sticky" by the board moderator.

- **Search the boards for specific question words**. I like to search for anything using the words: "what, how, and which." You may get a lot of results; scan through for anything that catches your eye. Look for posts that have TONS of views and replies.

- **Contribute to the board.** After a couple weeks of commenting, and being a non-spammy member, you could post a thread that asks people for their biggest questions about the topic. (Do this subtly, don't be a spammy self-promoter.)

The other cool thing about being an actual contributor to the board, before you write your book, is that when your book does come out, you'll have a HUGE collection of folks who'll be happy to read your book and leave you a review.

## Kick-Ass Research Source No.6: Your Story

Now, this one may seem off-topic. But one thing

I like to do when writing a book is spend ten minutes a day journaling about my personal experience, and how it relates to the topic I'm writing about.

This does two things:

- Makes your research more personal
- Gives you cool anecdotes and stories you can use in your writing.

Does the fact I spent years writing crappy SEO articles about prom dresses and Celtic tattoos have anything to do with writing a book? No...not directly.

But using that anecdote in the prologue of THIS book you're reading, was a quick illustration of how life-changing writing a non-fiction book can be...

And how awesome and kick-ass the self-publishing times we're living in are right now. (Which, I hope, made you feel more invested in what we were going to talk about.)

So, as you fill up your research bin, take a couple

minutes each day and riff on your own connection to the factoids you're collecting. I've found the work I do with this journaling research is often my reader's favorite stuff in my books.

# Chapter 4 Key Takeaways:

- **Research is awesome.** It kills clichés and lets you stand out from the rest of the crap.

- **Research can be a rabbit's hole.** Don't do too much. Readers want results, not every single fact about a book topic.

- **Looking at the Table of Contents for books in your field can be a great way to learn what most authors are doing.** Pay attention to what they do and do not focus on.

- **Skim the top two or three books in your area of concern.** Read the prologue and first chapter and then skim through the rest looking for any action steps or subheads.

- **Check out the book reviews for the top five books in your field**. This will key you into what people are REALLY looking for from a book on this subject.

- **Google Alerts is a super quick and easy way to become an expert.** Be sure your alerts are specific.

- **Message boards and forums are perfect for finding the hot-button questions your readers want answered.** Be a contributor to the forum and you can use that later on for book promotional stuff.

- **Journaling about your connection to the material can give you valuable stuff for your book.** Look for stories and anecdotes that help illustrate a point or strategy.

# Chapter 5:

# The Ultimate Guide to a Kick-Ass (and Super-Marketable) Book Title

*"Where is human nature so weak as in the bookstore."*
*- Henry Ward Beecher*

It's hard to overstate how important your book title is. (And how much a crappy title can hurt sales.)

The problem is, your book title has to do a hell of a lot of work. (Like a single parent working three jobs to make ends meet.)

Your book title has to:

- Promise what your book will deliver to the reader
- Show your tone, voice, and attitude as an author
- Cut through the clutter of a crowded book marketplace
- Use SEO-friendly keywords to boost discover-ability
- Handle 99% of the marketing for your book

It's difficult coming up with a title that can wear all those hats. (A fact underscored by the sheer amount of AWFUL titles out there.)

But it's not impossible.

And by nailing down a killer book title BEFORE you write your book, you can give your project the focus and momentum it needs to reach the finish line. (Not to mention a HUGE boost when it comes time to sell the damn thing.)

So, here are my FIVE KEYS to a Kick-Ass Title

that grabs would-be readers and turns lukewarm customers into die-hard fanatics:

# Kick-Ass Title Key No.1: Spy on the Competition

What better place to start than checking out what crappy titles your fellow non-fiction authors are using?

In my experience, I find MOST non-fiction book titles are:

- Boring
- Safe
- Vague

So why the hell are you looking at these? Well, you'll get a sense of the general vibe and tone of most books in your field. (And what vibe and tone isn't being represented.)

For my Punk Rock Marketing series I noticed most of the books in the Social Media Marketing space had titles like "Engage" and "Being Authentic" and "The Social Media Handbook." (Coma-inducing.)

So I went the other way, with titles like "Twitter Marketing That Doesn't Suck" and "Facebook Marketing That Doesn't Suck."

Nailing these titles early gave me a distinct marketing advantage and a clear tonal direction the books should strive toward. (Which was an edgy attitude that didn't waste time with fluff.)

*Action Step: Collect the titles of the top ten to fifteen books in your field. Look for discernible patterns, and what's NOT being expressed.*

## Kick-Ass Title Tip No.2: Embrace Your Inner Keyword Ninja

As artistic as we'd like to be, we still have to produce books that readers can find. (And buy.)

And there's NO better, faster, more effective way to ensure your book is found by the book-buying world than by using search-engine friendly keywords in your title.

Here's why keywords are so frickin' important:

- Your book's keywords determine how visible your book shows up in the **internal Amazon search engine**.
- Your book's keywords determine how visible your book is in the **Google search engine results**. (I can rank my books much higher than websites that spend thousands of dollars on their SEO campaigns.)
- Your book's keywords determine how many **pages on Amazon** your book will show up. This includes those "Customers Also Bought" and themed pages.

And of all the keywords associated with your

book, the most important is your title.

Now, before you freak out and think you have to generate your titles with some pre-ordained Google algorithm that makes you sound like a robot, there is an art to this. And an easy way to make your title sound cool.

We've all seen crudely titled books on Amazon stuffed to the gills with keywords. ("The Facts About Autism - 10 Facts About Autism," "Twitter Marketing - Twitter Marketing Tips You Should Know," "SEO Tips - Search Engine Optimization Tips")

Would you want to read any of those coma-inducing titles?

The crude strategy these authors use often works and gets those titles visibility. They're just never able to build up a reliable audience because their content sucks royal ass.

The trick is to use their own devious plan against them. (Kind of like The Man of Steel did at the end of *Superman II.* )

All you do is:

- **Google the phrase "Google Keyword Planner" — choose the first result.** You may need to create a Google AdWords account for this. Worry not, it's FREE

- **Under the "search for a new keyword"** field, throw in a bunch of words and phrases related to your book topic and click "Get ideas."

- **Select the "keyword ideas" tab.**

- **Click on the "average monthly searches"** button (this organizes all the searches by search volume).

- **Click "add to plan" for all the relevant keywords** that get at least 1000 searches a month

- **When you're done, click on the "download button"** in the lower right and your keywords will collect into a handy-dandy excel sheet.

*Action Step: Collect ten to twenty awesome keywords that can serve as a foundation for your book title.*

Because once you've got your list of juicy SEO keywords, you're now ready for...

## Kick-Ass Title Tip No.3: Find Your Place on Mt. Rushmore

There's a horrible term marketing "experts" like to use called brand differentiation. (I know, cringe-worthy, right?)

All it means it's more important (and profitable as an author) to be **different**, than **better**.

What's the best way to find out how you're DIFFERENT from your fellow authors? Simple, ask yourself the following questions:

- **What's my personality?** Are you the

"encouraging, make complex things easy teacher" guy? Or are you the "No-holds barred, tell it like it is, biker" girl?

- **How can I connect THAT personality to a void in the market?** Most titles are so boring, having ANY personality is bold. But bonus points if you can find a space where your book title can distinguish itself.

- **What language would best resonate with my ideal reader?** "Twitter Marketing That Doesn't Suck" worked for my social media marketing books. Wouldn't work so well if I was giving tips to faith-based charities. Think about the vibe you'd like your book to represent.

*Action Step: Answer the three questions above to hone in on what you'd like the tone, vibe and personality of your book to be.*

# Kick-Ass Title Tip No.4: Put It All in a Blender

Now you've got your ever-valuable keyword list and a feel for your place in the market, it's now time to put it all together in something I'm calling…

The Ultimate Book Title Blender!

All you do is take:

- **Two parts powerful SEO-friendly keyword.** Example: "How to Write a Book" gets 14K searches a month. Nice!

- **Three parts kick-ass title phrase that shows your personality.** Example: The phrase "That Doesn't Suck and Will Actually Sell" shows, I hope, that I'll shoot straight, and we'll have fun in the process.

- **Add a subtitle if needed.** I felt I had to add the subtitle "Ultimate, NO B.S. Guide to Writing a Non-Fiction Book" so as not to mislead folks looking to write the next Great American Novel.

And Presto! You've got a kick-ass book title!

Now, for finding a keyword to base your title around, here are a few tips:

- **Try to go with phrases at least three to four words long**. I've learned, the hard way, it's much easier to rank for a term like "How to Write a Book" than it is for a term like "Kindle Publishing." More words = more better!

- **Opt for phrases that get at least 1,000 searches a month**. This isn't a hard-fast rule, but it will keep you from spending a ton of time on a keyword that won't pay dividends.

- **Choose a keyword with low competition.** Another lesson I learned the hard way. I wrote a book called

"Search Engine Optimization That Doesn't Suck." Well, it turns out everyone and their brother had "Search Engine Optimization" in their title. (No bueno.) I changed it to "Search Engine Marketing That Doesn't Suck" and my sales skyrocketed.

And for the cool kick-ass title phrase that adds a little bit of personality to your title this will depend on your industry.

But here are two stand-bys I've used:

- **"That Doesn't Suck"** (Example: "How to Write a Book That Doesn't Suck") - Can be used in any market, with any subject. It offends quite a few people; I've got the emails to prove it. But it helps me stand out.

- **"Made Easy"** (Example: "Kindle Publishing Made Easy") - The nice part about this one is that everybody wants things made easy for them. Add this to your trusty keyword for instant title awesomeness.

- **"Tips and Tricks"** (Example: "Twitter Marketing Tips and Tricks") - Again, there's something about "tips and tricks" that sounds done-for-you. (Which everybody wants.)

- **"Hacks," "Secrets," "101," "Insider's Guide,"** and anything that sounds like insider info - People love secrets and things that give them info other people don't know.

The key is to experiment with this. Come up with different combinations. See what fits best with your personality.

The biggest sin is to come up with a title that doesn't fit in with how you plan to approach the book or doesn't deliver on its promise.

I know a guy who titled his book "How to Cure Autism." Yeah, uh, good keyword… but quite a lofty claim he couldn't deliver. (He got reamed by bad reviews and had to pull the book down.)

*Action Step: Come up with ten different title combinations that use BOTH your juicy keyword AND a variety of personality add- on phrases.*

## Kick-Ass Title Tip No.5: Pitch It

Once you've got your list of titles, the only thing left to do is to take them to your inner circle and find out which one they like best.

You'll want to get a cross-section of people. Here's who I ask:

- Friends and family
- Facebook connections
- Fellow writers
- Fellow message board members
- Employees at my local bookstore

Yes, I drive down to my neighborhood Barnes and Noble and ask the booksellers which title they like best. They deal with book titles all day long and can give you some of the sharpest insight and what separates the good from the bad.

In my experience, it's always the titles where I took a chance, where I took a stand and made it clear who the book was NOT for, that people responded to.

# Chapter 5 Key Takeaways:

- **A good title means a hell of a lot to the eventual success of your book.** That's because titles do so much, including help your book show up in the search engines, stick out from the competition and turn browsers into die-hard fans.

- **Start your title research by finding out what the competition is doing.** Most titles suck but find out what is — and is not — being conveyed in the other titles in your field.

- **Don't skip keywords. (Especially if writing non-fiction.)** Use the FREE Google keyword tool to find phrases that get at least 1,000 local searches a month, and brainstorm ways to incorporate them into your title.

- **Find out what unique way you can**

**contribute to the field of your book.** Brainstorm ways to use your personality into a compelling author brand.

- **Combine an SEO-friendly keyword with a unique gotcha phrase (such as Tips, Hacks, and Insider's Guide) to create a compelling, kick-ass title.** Make sure the title sounds human and doesn't promise something your book won't cover.

- **Test the awesomeness of your book title by trying it out on members of your inner tribe.** Don't forget to include your local bookseller to get their input.

# Chapter 6:

# Building the Perfect Beast (Book Outlining Made Easy)

*"He who cannot limit himself will never know how to write."*

— *Nicholas Boileau*

I hate the term "outlining."

It sounds boring and dry and something anal writers do with Excel spreadsheet formulas and a cultish devotion to figure out everything single thing they will say before they say it.

And, instead, for years I wrote from my "gut."

I'd churn out reams of florid prose and biting commentary — hopped up on overpriced lattes and day-old bran muffins — figuring I didn't need to outline, because I "knew" my subject. I had done my research.

I'd just "figure it out" along the way.

But after hitting a wall mid-way through my THIRD book project, I realized the "gut" is great at emotion, creativity and innovation. (All the reasons writing is so damn much fun.)

What the gut ain't terribly good at is:

- Knowing EXACTLY what readers are looking for
- Knowing EXACTLY what readers aren't looking for
- Knowing how many chapters your book NEEDS to cover the material
- Knowing how long each chapter should be
- Knowing the best way to sequence your

information

- Knowing when to STOP

I'd still be hunched over my laptop at my local Starbucks, trying to mold my latest project into something coherent, if it weren't for my mentor and friend, an Uber successful self-published author, who said:

"Good writing isn't in the words you use, it's in answering the right questions."

And nothing helps you answer the right questions, and write quicker and more effectively, than a good outline.

So, here are my 5 Steps to Building a Creative & Killer Book Outline that'll have your non-fiction tome structured and kicking serious ass in no time:

## Book Outline Step No.1: Do the Math

I know. You're a writer. You hate Math.

But this is Math that can help you out — unlike

that crappy Geometry class Mr. Flattum taught —
because it tells you:

- How many chapters you should include in your book?
- How long you should make your chapters?
- How long your book should be in total words?

Now, this will all depend on the breadth and scope of your subject. I try to shoot for a **finished book length of 10,000 to 20,000 words**. Anything longer than 20,000 words and I'll break it off into a second book.

So, if I know that 10,000 words is my absolute minimum to producing a book-length work, then my Math will look something like this:

- Prologue & Epilogue — 500 words a piece (1,000 words total)

- Eight chapters — 1,000 words a piece (8,000 words total)
- Extra goodies — 1,000 words (1,000 words total)

Now these aren't iron-clad rules. I don't ALWAYS include an Epilogue. I don't ALWAYS stick to the 1,000-word chapter lengths. (I write chapters in the 1,000-1,500-word range; but your particular rhythm may differ.)

And I often have WAY over 1,000 words of extra goodies that come up in writing.

But this is just a road map. It gives me a rough idea of what I need to shoot for — about eight to ten chapters, or sub topics, to organize my kick-ass content around. (And my impossible, super-hard task of writing a book has become… well… do-able.)

*Action Step: Break out the calculator (or abacus) and figure out the minimum number of chapters and words you'd like to shoot for with your book.*

# Book Outline Step No.2: Begin With the End in Mind

This is a simple step, but one often overlooked by many authors. You need to ask yourself: What RESULT do I want my readers to achieve by reading my book?

Is it to lose weight? Have a better relationship with their troubled teen? Learn some awesome vegetarian recipes?

They are not reading your book to appreciate your fine liberal-arts education or dazzle in your intellect. They want a result, they want knowledge, they want SOMETHING to be different. (Even if it's as simple as adding a gluten-free chili dish to their repertoire.)

And the clearer and more concise you can be with this statement, the clearer and more concise your book will be.

I used to work in the film business, and my boss would often say "if somebody can't write the plot of their film on a post-it note, they don't KNOW what their film is about."

Same goes for your book.

*Action Step: Write down the end result you think your ideal readers want after they read your book.*

# Book Outline Step No.3: Ask the Right (and Wrong) Questions

This is where you win the battle for a good book. (Or lose.)

Not in the admiral's tent, where you devise strategy and give orders, but in the actual trenches where your readers live and breathe each day.

That's because even the most beautifully written chapter in the world is worthless if it's NOT connected to the conversation already going on in the head of your reader.

And how do we perform this bit of self-publishing clairvoyance?

We figure out what questions your readers are

already asking… and then we make damn sure we answer them.

The best way to do this is to scan your research and look for:

- Questions mentioned — again and again — in message boards or forums
- Blog posts with the words "How" or "why" Or "What"
- Technical sub-topics that might confuse a good portion of your readers
- Areas that a majority of your fellow authors have covered in their books
- Common complaints in relevant Amazon book reviews
- Any source of confusion or strong emotion related to your topic

Once you've looked over your research, write out these sub-topics in question form. Again, this will depend on the experience and knowledge of your ideal reader.

If I'm doing a book to help IT professionals with their job networking, I don't think I need to include - "What is a Blog?" (Unless I'm speaking to the world's most clueless IT guy.)

But I might want to include things like:

- What Should (and Shouldn't) You Put on Your Personal Blog?
- What's the Best Way to Approach a Recruiter?

- How Do You Handle a Layoff on Your Resume?

And how many questions do you need to come up with?

Well, I like to shoot for at least twelve. This forces me to dig deep and come up with interesting questions I might not have thought of.

*Action Step: Look over your research and write the top*

*twelve to fifteen questions your readers have about your book topic on index cards.*

## Book Outline Step No.4: Build Your Frankenstein Monster

So you've got at least twelve kick-ass questions written on index cards. Now it's time to:

Put your index cards in logical sequence

Write three tips or strategies related to each question on the back of each card

For instance, in my Facebook Marketing example, under the topic question "How Do I Get Facebook Followers" I've got:

- Comment on other pages
- Run a Facebook ad
- Insert a "follow me on Facebook" link in my email signature

For the question "How Do I Nail my Phone Interview" I've got:

- Create a quiet environment (No dogs, no kids, no zombies)
- Open all relevant company info on my desktop browser tabs
- Stand & Smile (Makes your voice sound more confident)

You don't have to go into extreme detail with these; you want to see if the question/chapter topic is strong enough to be on its own AND whether you have any research blind spots you need to fill in.

And as for the order of the cards, do what seems logical. Think about taking your reader on a journey, from uneducated newbie to (moderate) expert.

If you were doing something on Twitter marketing, you'd want to start with question cards like "How do I set up my profile?" or "Isn't Twitter a big old waste of time?" before answering questions like "How do I schedule my tweets with 3rd-party software?"

*Action Step: Arrange your twelve to fifteen question cards in order. Write three tips or supporting points on the back of each card to help illustrate answers to that specific question.*

## Book Outline Step No.5: Cut the Fat (and Move the Good Stuff)

I think it was Elmore Leonard who said the key to writing was to "Skip the boring parts." And that works doubly well for your non-fiction book.

So, look over your topic index cards and look for ways to:

- **Cut out obvious topics** (in the beginning) that delay the start of what your reader wants to learn. (In the film business they call this "throat clearing" and it can be the death of your book.)

- **Combine chapter topics into one larger, more comprehensive topic**. (Do you need two chapters on how to choose the right golf club? Maybe not.)
- **Remove any question/chapter topics that are tangents** and hurt the reader get to their intended result.
- **Remove any topics too advanced for your ideal readership**. (You may know a lot about thermodynamics, but it doesn't mean it's a good fit for your book on changing a water heater)
- **Move topics around** to find the best sequential fit.

You don't want to rush this step, trust me. It may take you extra time, but if you're able to lock down a cohesive order of topics — and remove the boring, weaker ones from the mix — it will make your actual composition much, much easier. (And way more kick-ass.)

This doesn't mean you're locked into the order, or topics, that you choose at this stage. I changed (and re-arranged) the topics of this book quite a few times during writing.

But you need something to get started. And having a coherent list of chapter topics, with the boring ones thrown out, is a great first step.

*Action Step: Scan your twelve to fifteen topic cards and try to cut them down to eight to ten topics.*

# Chapter 6 Key Takeaways:

- **Outlining is not just for left-brained anal writers who have no creativity.** It's the most freeing thing you can do for your creativity.

- **Outline by working out the numbers for your book.** I shoot for eight to ten chapters, 1,000 words a piece, with a prologue and epilogue of 500 words a piece, thrown in.

- **Before brainstorming chapter topics nail down the result** you want your reader to have at the end of reading your book. Make this clear (but) powerful.

- **Come up with a list of the top twelve to fifteen questions your reader has about the topic you're writing about.** Look at message boards, blog posts, confusing sub-topics, and Amazon book review complaints for inspiration.

- **Put your twelve to fifteen questions in order, and for each question write three tips or strategies on the book.** This will help you determine what's worthy of a whole chapter. (And what you might need to go back and do research on.)

- **Remove questions that are boring, obvious, overly-advanced or not interesting.** Spend time working on the best sequence of topics that will take your reader from clueless to locked-in.

# Chapter 7:

# How to Write Books People Love (and Will Help You Sell)

*"Simple's the most sophisticated thing of all."*
*—Ina Garten*

You've got your kick-ass book idea, enough background research to get started, and a rough idea of the eight to ten chapter topics you'll be covering in your fabulous non-fiction tome.

Must mean you're ready to churn out those words to your masterpiece?

Well, not quite.

See, just because we know WHAT a specific

chapter will cover, doesn't mean we know HOW to write that chapter.

Because the art of writing a great non-fiction book — that leads to consistent sales over time — is REALLY about mastering one simple art: walking your reader through an idea in a clear and concise way that makes them not feel like an idiot.

And for years I screwed this up.

I'd spend weeks writing and rewriting (what I thought) was the best and most comprehensive prose of my life. Turned out it confused my readers.

And I would have given up the whole "writing for a living" thing if I hadn't stumbled upon a simple system that not only simplified my writing process and helped me create more coherent and focused work, but also led to a huge boost in recurring sales. (And a cult following.)

Would you like to know the system? Ya ready to have a cult following? (Let's make you a minor non-fiction celebrity, shall we?)

# "Is Our Children Learning?"

I wish I could take credit for this system. ('Fraid I'm not that smart.)

I got it from Internet Marketing guru Eben Pagan who has made over 100 million dollars selling information products online for the last ten years. (Don't hold it against him; despite the resume, he's a cool guy.)

I believe he got the system from even smarter people at Harvard, who spend all day drinking Earl Grey tea and reading about breezy topics such as "The Cognitive Learning Systems of the Human Brain."

So, here's the gist of what the Harvard crew found out about the way us humans gain new information: We don't all learn things the same way.

If you're a parent or a teacher — or have taught guitar lessons to cynical, emo suburban teenagers named Trevor (like I have) — then you'll know this to be true.

Some people need to know WHY they need to learn something before they dig into the details. (I'm in this category, I need to know the big picture, how it affects me, before I become invested in something.)

Others need to understand the WHAT: the pros and cons, the various theories, the complete step-by-step journey from beginning-to-end.

Other people you need to tell what to do. They don't care about theories or ideas or knowledge. They want to know HOW they can achieve their result right away. (Without thinking too much.)

Each of them are trying to get the same result but have very different approaches to learning.

And here's the crazy thing: if you create written content that doesn't cater to each of these learning biases, then you risk alienating a HUGE section of your readership. (Which can impact your sales, through lukewarm reviews and lack of buzz.)

So, how do we handle this? Do we write three different versions of the same book? Good Lord, no!

We follow the same, exact structure I've been using for the FIRST SIX chapters of this book. (And which I'd like you to rip off for your own book.)

## The Power of the "Why, What, How" Formula

You might have noticed that each of the chapters in this book followed the same structure:

- **Brief introduction to the topic the chapter will cove**r… the WHY it's important you're reading what you're reading.
- **Step-by-step series of tips or strategies to help educate the reader about that topic**… the WHAT the reader needs to know.
- **Series of action steps (or takeaways) that somebody could follow right**

**away**... the HOW they can act now

This wasn't by accident. By presenting your information in this way it achieves four important things:

- Ensures I leave no single learning system out of the loop
- Gives each chapter a coherent thematic focus (Less chance for you to ramble)
- Reinforces the same idea repeatedly (In a way that doesn't make you sound repetitive)
- Builds genuine trust between you and the reader (Because a majority of the readers will GET what you're saying)

How you balance these three elements (the WHY, the WHAT, the HOW) will depend on the topic and the audience for your book.

In this book you're reading, I've LEANED

heavily on the WHY sections — this is because there are quite a few big-picture ideas that are important for writing a book. (Example: Why research is important, often used as a crutch to not get written and easier than you might think.)

But for a topic whose WHY is damn obvious — such as "getting more email subscribers" or "formatting a screenplay correctly" — I will tilt the balance more toward the WHAT section.

And again, this ain't physics, there's no hard-fast rule about how much time to spend in each section. But by making sure you spend a minimum of time in each of these three elements you'll ensure it fulfils your number one job as a writer which is reader comprehension.

So, now I've let you peek behind the curtain and see who the "Wizard" is, here's a more in-depth look at the three elements of the WHY, WHAT and HOW and how you can use them to write your chapters effortlessly.

# Element No.1: The WHY

This part of the chapter answers one fundamental question: WHY the hell should the reader care?

Suppose I'm writing a book on setting up a blog and I've got a chapter on FTP (File Transfer Protocol) and my chapter starts like this:

*"First, you download Filezilla. Second, you type in your FTP settings. Third, drag your header image to the root folder of your blog…"*

You'd probably be like "Whoa! Wait a minute! What the hell are we talking about?!"

That's because I skipped the WHY and went straight for the WHAT. (A common, but sometimes lethal, non-fiction book error.)

But if instead I started this way:

*"FTP (File Transfer Protocol) is a horrible name for something that is important for blog publishers to learn.*

*"Not only can it save you time and money — no need to wait on your webmaster to upload that new header of yours —*

*but it can also be a lifesaver in the event someone hacks your website. (Which will happen. Trust me.)"*

Suddenly you're interested.

Not because you give a crap about the science of file sharing — would you believe there are people who find it interesting? — but because it can save you time and money and the huge headache of recovering your hacked files.

Now, here are a few tips when writing out your WHY section:

- **Don't go too long here**. I wish I was better at this myself as you can tell. But try to get in and get out as soon as you can.

- **Don't go too short.** You want the WHY to be crystal clear. Don't be cute or clever here about the WHY. Spell it out.

- **Try to connect the WHY to a benefit, not a feature**. You are not selling a hammer, you are selling the hole in the wall that lets people hang that nice photo of the kids. People don't care about the technical details, they care about the cool thing they'll get from knowing what you're teaching them.

- **Personal anecdotes are good**. As long as you don't go on and on. Keep it connected to the over-arching point of the chapter.

- **Always end with some kind of sentence that points the way to the WHAT section**. "Here are the seven big strategies/five key tips/three central pillars…to help you do that thing you want to do and rule the world."

## Element No.2: The WHAT

This is the meat of your chapter. This is where you get to flaunt your expertise.

Where you walk your reader, step-by-step

through what they need to know about a specific topic.

Now, you'll notice, in this book, I use A LOT of numbers to break up my tips, strategies, steps, elements, etc. That's because people LOVE numbers. (Especially odd numbers, God knows why.)

Maybe there's something about knowing how many "somethings" a reader has to endure to get a result that makes the brain more comfortable.

You DON'T have to use numbers. You could use subheads or themed sections or Disney characters or whatever you want.

Make sure you break up the WHAT in some easily digested format. Having huge blocks of text, with no headings, will overwhelm readers and cause them to skim.

When you're writing your WHAT, here's a few things to help keep you on track:

- **Walk people through from beginning**

**to end**. Don't start with a more advanced step and then double back to the beginning. It will confuse folks.

- **Don't neglect a first step even if it seems obvious to you.** I'm guilty of this as much as the next writer. Take the temperature of your ideal reader; if you can't assume they already know how to do something - like set up a Facebook page or change the oil of their 1976 Lincoln — then you've got to put it in your WHAT.

- **Include any common obstacles or anger zones that might befall the reader — and that happened to you or others.** Makes them feel like they're getting the inside scoop, and they'll love you for it.

- **Mention any contrary theories or opinions that might refute a particular**

**strategy or technique you're discussing**. I did this with the Ezine Articles section in Chapter 4. (How MOST non-fiction book guides tell you it's okay to use crappy article directories as research.) Builds your credibility, big time.

- **Don't overload the reader with a TON of tips or strategies in a single chapter**. Seven to ten is my max. Any more than that and think about breaking up the topic into two separate chapter topics.

- **If you can, try to make the last strategy/step give the reader a real sense of accomplishment**. This is where they turn on the faucet and see the new sink valve they installed, working. This is where they create that ad campaign that gets them 2,000 new Facebook fans. This is where they get the last piece of the puzzle to FINALLY write that kick-ass non-fiction book of theirs. (Yes, I'm talkin' to you!)

## Element No.3: The HOW

This one's simple. All you gotta do is summarize your big, major points and put them in a simple action step format that your reader can follow.

Trust me: for quite a few of your readers this will be the ONLY part of your book they read. (Sad, but true.) So, this is a good place for any:

- Major tips or strategies
- Resources, such as websites or books you mentioned
- Big things to avoid

And if you follow this simple formula with your chapter topics, the WHY, WHAT, and HOW, you'll find not only are you selling WAY MORE books, but you'll soon be gaining that most rare thing of all. A die-hard reader who will devour everything you write.

# Chapter 7 Key Takeaways:

- **People learn stuff in different ways**. Your books will resonate with a majority of readers if you include the WHY, WHAT and HOW of a topic in every chapter you write.

- **The WHY (first section) is where you discuss the big-picture ideas around a specific topic.** Personal anecdotes are good as long as they don't run long. Just be clear about what you'll present, and why it's important.

- **The WHAT (second section) is where you walk your reader step-by-step through solving the problem or answering the question of the chapter.** Good stuff here includes theories, techniques, alternate opinions, and insider strategies the reader will need to approach a topic.

- **The HOW (third section) is a simple list of action steps the reader can do right now to achieve their result.** Don't get cute with these. Be clear and give your readers the least they need to know.

# Chapter 8:

# 6 Tips for Writing Your Damn Book

*"Perfection is the enemy of excellence"*
*—Voltaire*

So, what now?

You've got a rough outline, a list of the most important questions your reader needs answered, and a structure to use when writing chapters. Now it's just a matter of, as good old Mr. Hemingway said, to "sitting down at the typewriter and opening a vein."

But having started — and never finished —

more non-fiction books than anybody I know, I can tell you that the journey toward book completion can be fraught with peril and nagging self-doubt.

And it's EASY for someone to tell you to just "keep writing" and "stick with it," but that can be difficult when you've never completed a project this ambitious before.

So, before you give up your dream and drown yourself in a carton of Ben & Jerry's Cherry Garcia, here are my Top 5 Tips to Push Through Self-Doubt and Get Your Damn Book Written:

# Kick-Ass Writing Tip No.1: Map Out Your Schedule

Trust me, I'm no left-brained, anal, super prompt scheduler person. But learning to map out and schedule my writing was the number one key becoming a professional writer, and not some literary wannabe.

And not because it has anything to do with time

management — I always wonder what Einstein would think of that term. No, it's because scheduling your book makes it do-able in your crazy, creative brain. (The only place it counts.)

If I were to ask you RIGHT NOW to have a ten-thousand-word book completed in three weeks, your amygdala (the fight-or-flight part of your brain) would freak out and try to come up with a hundred different reasons you couldn't/shouldn't do it. ("I don't have time," "I'm not ready," "There's too many episodes of Law and Order in my TiVo,"… anything to help you avoid crippling fear.)

But if I tell you, all you got to do is write five hundred words a day — about a page and a half — for three weeks and you'll have your first book done… it's not so impossible.

It might even be do-able. (Especially if you've already done the research, and you know what you're gonna write about already.)

And making it do-able in your mind is 75% of the challenge of writing a book.

# Kick-Ass Writing Tip No.2: Keep Your Sessions Short, But Frequent

I remember the first book project I tackled.

I came up with this brilliant plan where I'd write a book in a single weekend, by blocking off four hours each Saturday and Sunday. (This would help me reach my modest goal of completing fifty books a year — two weeks off for Christmas, I'm no workaholic — without missing a single episode of The Deadliest Catch.)

Yeah, well, you know what happened.

I spent the first hour, that Saturday, tweaking and re-tweaking one paragraph and then gave up later that afternoon. (Figuring there was something wrong with my brain chemistry or my caffeine intake.) When I had put so much pressure on myself in those weekend sessions I had set myself up for failure.

Don't do this.

I recommend you shoot for SHORT, but

frequent writing sessions. If that means fifteen minutes that's okay. If that means two sessions of ten minutes that's okay.

If that means you can only spare five minutes a day, then that's okay too. (Chances are you'll gain momentum and want to keep going. Which is a good thing.)

Just try to write everyday if you can. I know it can be hard with real life banging up against the door of your office. But cranking out words every day will not only help you develop the writing habit, but it will also keep you from wearing out.

## Kick-Ass Writing Tip No.3: Don't Edit (Until the Rewrite)

Just because we're writing non-fiction doesn't mean we aren't creative. When you're churning out your pages, it's helpful if you can tell your critical, thinking, anal left-brain to take a sabbatical.

Not a permanent vacation; you'll need that

critical mind when you're rewriting. But when you're composing a rough draft you're trying things out, you're throwing crap against the wall and seeing what will stick. You're trying to find your "voice," and the best way to say the things you need to say.

And editing or revising as you complete your first draft is a recipe for stuffing that "voice" at the bottom of the closet. (And it's your "voice" that will connect with readers.)

So, try your best, to save all that self-loathing and merciless criticism for the rewriting phase. (Plenty of time to hate yourself then.)

## Kick-Ass Writing Tip No.4: Fix It in Post

There's an expression in the film biz. (Where I spent a few years reading awful screenplays about zombie aliens blowing up the White House.)

If something isn't right during a film shoot — maybe the cinematographer didn't get the right shot, or that coked-up diva actress went AWOL — then often the director will say we'll "fix it in post." (Meaning we can clear up any issues in post-production, so let's not stop shooting NOW.)

The same is true with your book. Whatever obstacle or hiccup or research blind spot you HIT with your book can be fixed in post.

This can be as simple as a section that needs more research, a chapter opening that feels forced, a strategy or technique that needs more explanation. A chapter title that's as dull as a Nicholas Sparks novel.

Whatever it is, you can always build it out later.

What I'll do, when I'm writing and hit a bump in the road, is I'll write: "Need stats here" or "Insert personal anecdote" or "Put Action steps."

Whatever I do, I try not to stop. Which is…

## Kick-Ass Writing Tip No.5: Don't Stop (Till You Finish)

Trust me: I speak from LOTS of experience on

this topic. If you stop in the middle of a project, you will NEVER finish.

Oh, I know you think you will. I know you think you'll get back to it. You need to do more research or re-do your chapter topics or come up with a different title...

But that's just your amygdala trying to get you to do anything that isn't SCARY. (Because the amygdala hates anything that's scary. And writing is scary!)

The psychic energy it takes to resurrect a stalled project is so HIGH it can take a Herculean effort to get it up and running. And if you're somewhat new to writing, it won't happen. (Mark Twain nearly gave up on *Huckleberry Finn* half-way through. And he was frickin' Mark Twain.)

So, whatever you do, just finish. I don't care if you wrote the worst book since Paris Hilton's autobiography — no chance you did — just finish! You will learn so much more about your book, your process and yourself if you keep going to the end.

# Kick-Ass Writing Tip No. 6: Focus on Output, Not the Day-to-Day

You will hit a point when you write some less-than stellar prose. Where the writing feels stilted, awkward and insincere.

You'll think: "Why the hell did I ever think I could do this? I'm the worst writer since that woman who wrote those awful Twilight books... and those are the worst books ever written."

It's at moments like that when it's important to remind yourself that you and I are like professional athletes. (Without the entourage and luxury sports cars.) No ONE day will make or break our reputation.

Just because we had a crappy day of writing doesn't mean we won't kick ass tomorrow. Today we could write the best prose since William Faulkner — just with more paragraph breaks — and it won't guarantee we won't lay a huge turd on the page tomorrow.

The key is to resist the temptation to judge your writing talent on a day-to-day basis. This is difficult. We are writers, and so are prone to judging ourselves like the Spanish Inquisition.

But try to realize that as long as you are putting down words, whether it be 250, 500 or 100 a day... that you are on track.

And that everything you find wrong with your writing is fixable. (But only if you finish the damn thing.)

## Kick-Ass Writing Tip No.7: Save the Prologue and Epilogue for Later

These are important, as readers love them, and they set the tone and mission statement for your book.

Until you crank out your first draft, you don't know what your mission statement is. (And you'll just be wasting time and energy on a section you'll end up rewriting anyway.)

So save yourself the added emotional turmoil and skip these vital sections until after you've got a first draft on the books. (I'll go over prologues and epilogues in the last chapter.)

# Chapter 8 Key Takeaways:

- **Work out a writing schedule for your book.** Break it down by day to see your book project is realistic and not impossible.

- **Skip the marathon writing sessions, and go for the quick, daily writing bursts.** Doesn't matter if it's ten minutes or a half-hour, try to keep your writing sessions short, but daily.

- **Don't edit while you're writing your rough draft.** Nothing will stall your project quicker than looking over your work before it's complete.

- **If something is missing, fix it later.** Just make a note of what a section needs, such as more research or a new chapter, and resolve yourself to fix it in your second draft.

- **Keep writing until you finish that first draft.** You will never finish it if you stop. Trust me. Don't make me come to your house and rough you up. Just finish the damn thing!

- **Realize no single day of writing will define you.** Reputations are made over the long haul, not over one writing session. Keep track of your weekly output, not your daily performance.

- **Ditch writing your prologue and epilogue until after your first draft.** No need to summarize something that you haven't written.

# Chapter 9:

# 5 Ways to Rewrite Your Book Into a Super-Awesome Work of Art

*"I believe more in the scissors than I do in the pencil."*
*—Truman Capote*

I wasn't going to include this chapter. You bought this book to learn how to WRITE a book, not go through your manuscript looking for passive verbs.

But because I feel rewriting IS a big part of writing, and where your biggest improvements lurk, I wanted to share with you a few rewriting tips and tricks I've learned along the way.

So, without further ado (or any rewriting), here are my 5 Steps to Rewriting Awesomeness:

# Rewriting Step No.1: Take a Break (I Mean It!)

You'll want to put the finishing touches to your last chapter and INSTANTLY edit from page one.

Don't!

It's important you take a break and create some distance between you and the material. (Not to mention celebrate the fact you finished your book.) What you've done is something 99% of the world talks about wanting to do, but never does. And you did it! So revel in your awesomeness and enjoy this moment.

After six or seven days of Hemingway-esque debauchery — boy, doesn't that sound fun? — you can jump back in and paw at your manuscript and look for flaws and inconsistencies. (And there'll be a ton.)

But until then, put your manuscript away, let it collect dust on your desktop, and bask in the glow of knowing you can say: "I'm a Writer, dammit!"

## Rewriting Step No.2: Create a Rewriting Schedule

I used to dread rewriting. Felt like doing my taxes. (Something I knew I had to do but took every ounce of my mental and physical will to complete.)

And then a writing teacher clued me in that rewriting is a hell of a lot easier if each draft of your manuscript has one focus. Instead, of reading through your book and trying to fix everything that's wrong with it, from beginning-to-end, just devote each draft to a particular area of emphasis.

This can include simple things like, grammar, passive voice, source attributions — and more complex items like introductions, gaping research holes, etc.

Here's how I break it down in the rewriting process:

- **Draft 2 - Fix grammar** (Spell check, weird contractions, awkward phrasing.)
- **Draft 3 - Remove passive voice** (Kill them passive verbs and offending adverbs planted in your book)
- **Draft 4 - Strengthen the WHY sections** (Add personal stories and ensure your WHY is clear)
- **Draft 5 - Boost the WHAT sections** (Build out tips/strategies, if needed, and remove anything not related to topic)
- **Draft 6 - Clean Up the HOW sections**
- **Draft 7 - Add quotes**, references, citations and additional research

I see rewriting akin to setting the EQ when recording music. First you clean up the bass, make sure the low end doesn't feel muddled and isn't overpowering. Then slog your way up through the mids and to the high end, to make sure everything is in balance.

If you try to fix everything at once, you'll not only miss something, but it'll also make you feel you're not making any progress. (Which you are.)

## Rewriting Step No.3: Write Your Prologue and Epilogue

So now you've got your manuscript in better shape, and you have a clearer idea of what the hell you're trying to say, it's time to take aim at your Prologue and Epilogue.

I should say, you don't HAVE to write a prologue and epilogue. (Nobody is going to send you to non-fiction jail if you don't include these.)

But I like them because having a prologue and epilogue:

- Provides a nice bookend effect to the

whole book.

- Allows me to get in information not tied to a single thematic sub-topic.
- Gives me a chance, in the prologue, to provide a BIG WHY for the entire book. (Why I wrote this book, why people should read it, why people NEED to read it now!)
- Gives me a chance, in the epilogue, to detail HOW readers can take what they know to some higher level of achievement they may not have thought of.

If you read the prologue that started off this book — and you know who you are — you might have noticed I went considerably over the BIG WHYs of writing a book that doesn't suck.

Such as:

- **WHY write a book** (It can change your

life; it changed mine)

- **WHY write a book now** (It's never been easier to get your book published than ever before)

- **WHY this book can help** (I've been there, I've done it; I know what to do and what not to do and I'll try not to bore you)

And that's all there is to the prologue. You're trying to get people excited about what you will cover and invested in the material.

You're not going over specific tips and strategies they need to use. (Far too early for that.) You're just trying to lay the groundwork for what you hope to be a kick-ass writer/reader relationship.

The epilogue is much easier. (Is shorter.) But in other ways it's the most difficult part of the book. Because you are trying to say goodbye gracefully.

Here's what I try to do in every epilogue:

- **Remind the reader what they've accomplished** (They've gotten to the end, they deserve recognition)

- **Point the reader to where they can go from here** (Okay, they know all this stuff you've been teaching them, now what?)

- **Give them a sense of the BIG PICTURE** (It's not JUST about learning new stuff, it's about who they've become after learning this new stuff)

Now, this rah-rah, self-help style epilogue may not be appropriate for your market. If you're doing a book on "How to Get the Phone Number of Any Girl You Meet" you may not want to spend a ton of time on the REAL reason we crave human affection and company.

But I find, in all my different book markets, if I don't include a prologue and an epilogue I deprive my readers the joy of realizing they've done more than finish a book.

They've learned something that can change their lives.

# Rewriting Secret No.4: Get Thee to a Copy-editor

I will not spend a ton of time debating this point; you NEED to have somebody with fresh eyes go through your book like it's an IRS audit.

This is because you think you're making sense (when you actually aren't) AND you'll miss obvious grammatical errors. (That can ding you big time with reader reviews.)

Finding a good copy-editor is easy; I like to use a freelance site such as Upwork. (I have a regular copy-editor I work with whom charges me between $60-$75 dollars for each of my books she handles, depending on length. Which is a total bar-gain!)

But there are plenty of other places to find copy-editors. I've had success with Craigslist in finding local (cheap) editing talent. (I've also found scary people who should be hospitalized.)

What you do NOT want to do is to rely on yourself — trust me, you'll miss something — or rely on a friend or a fellow writer. You need somebody who has experience going through manuscripts line-by-line looking for the tiniest bit of grammatical oddity or unclear wording. (Doing this will boost your positive reviews, which puts money in your pocket.)

## Rewriting Secret No.5: Let It Go (and Send It Out)

Yes, you could follow in the footsteps of Dorothy Parker, who claimed () to have rewritten every word in her stories at least three times. But at some point, you gotta say: "Okay, time to publish this damn thing!"

How you'll know it's "ready for prime-time" is a personal decision. I find with my projects, after a week, I start fussing with minor, cosmetic things, such as the font styles and then I know it's time to upload that sucker and get it published.

The cool thing about self-publishing your book on a platform like Amazon's Kindle Publishing System, is that you can ALWAYS go back and make changes. (I do this all the time with my marketing stuff.)

But you want to make sure your book isn't sloppy or formatted badly. Forget perfection, just get it good enough, and then collect those well-earned royalties.

# Chapter 9 Key Takeaways:

- **Don't touch your book for a week after finishing the first draft**. Take a break from the writing process and celebrate your monumental victory. (Make sure you treat yourself with something indulgent.)

- **Break up your subsequent drafts by area of emphasis**. This includes grammar, passive voice, further research, and the WHY, WHAT and HOW sections.

- **Prologues are great for establishing the big WHY of the book**. Push the urgency and positive outcomes that'll come from reading the book.

- **Epilogues are great for giving readers a sense of the big picture**. Of what's possible, now they know what they know.

- **Hiring a copy-editor to look at your**

**manuscript is a must**. Find a quality copy-editor over at a site such as Upwork. This might be the best money you'll spend ever.

- **When you fuss with your book, after a couple weeks, upload it and work on your next book**. You can always go back and rewrite more later.

# Epilogue:
# The Greatest Epilogue You'll Ever Read

*"If you do the thing you fear, the death of fear is certain"*
—*Ralph Waldo Emerson*

If you read my spiel about prologues and epilogues in the last chapter, then you'll have a good idea of what I will share here.

I will congratulate you for reading this far. (And if you wrote your book to completion, then I will remind you of how much of a kick-ass rock star you are.)

I will also tell you what you should do next after completing your first book: Write more books.

Turn this ONE book into a second and a third and maybe even a fourth. (Then use the different volumes in your series to promote the collection.)

I'd also suggest you pursue other book markets — maybe look at some of those other book topics you haven't dug into yet.

That the more books you write… the quicker, better and more lucrative your writing craft becomes.

Not every book you write, or series you pursue, will be a Kindle bestseller. But if you keep at it, you'll get a gut instinct for which projects are worth spending time on. (And which projects, though they sound interesting, will not help you reach your goals of being a successful full-time writer.)

And all of this is true…

But the most important thing I want you to realize is that making a full-time living on Amazon book royalties is just the first step. It's a great first step, and one that will have you checking your Amazon sales dashboard like a teenager checking their Facebook page.

But soon, if you keep at it, and you put your heart and soul into these books the strangest thing will happen. Serious momentum will build around you and your brand.

People you've never met will recommend your book on Facebook. Thought leaders in your field will quote you in blog posts. Industry associations will ask you to come speak at their yearly conference. (First for free, then for actual hard currency.)

And before you know it, you're sharing your story with a group of total strangers, who are listening and taking notes about the **things you say,** all because YOU wrote a book.

Now I don't know what your eventual goal is with this whole writing thing. You may just want to see your byline on a published book. Or maybe you just want to make enough money to tell your supervisor to take his performance review and shove it up his ass.

But these books you're about to write can do wonderful things. I'm living proof. I only hope you and I can meet up someday at some writer's conference and we can laugh about all those crappy jobs we had...

Before we became the most awesome thing in the entire world. Somebody who writes words that other people pay to read.

Thank you SO MUCH for letting me guide you through this crazy, Book Writing Journey.

If you have questions, or you'd just like to drop me a line to let me know what you thought of this humble tome, you can ping me at: Michael@indiepubnation.com.

Good luck with your Book Writing Awesomeness!

And if you've enjoyed this book, or even if you didn't enjoy the book, would you be willing to leave a review?

Even a sentence or two really helps us indie authors carve out a career as a creative professional.

Head over to IndiePubNation.com/HowBook to leave a review on Amazon (and enjoy truckloads of good karma):

# A Special FREE Gift for You!

If you'd like FREE instant access to my seminar "5 Secrets to Making a Damn Good Living (As a Writer)" then head over to **ScriptBully.com/5secrets**. (What else you gonna do? Read another "Twilight" book?!)

**DISCLAIMER AND/OR LEGAL NOTICES:**
Every effort has been made to accurately represent this book and it's potential. Results vary with every individual, and your results may or may not be different from those depicted. No promises, guarantees or warranties, whether stated or implied, have been made that you will produce any specific result from this book. Your efforts are individual and unique, and may vary from those shown. Your success depends on your efforts, background and motivation.

The material in this publication is provided for educational and informational purposes only and is not intended as medical advice. The information contained in this book should not be used to diagnose or treat any illness, metabolic disorder, disease or health problem. Always consult your physician or health care provider before beginning any nutrition or exercise program. Use of the programs, advice, and information contained in this book is at the sole choice and risk of the reader.

Made in the USA
San Bernardino, CA
20 November 2019

60195135R00095